I AM KIND ONLINE

RACHAEL MORLOCK

PowerKiDS press.

NEW YORK

Published in 2020 by The Rosen Publishing Group, Inc.
29 East 21st Street, New York, NY 10010

First Edition

Editor: Elizabeth Krajnik
Book Design: Reann Nye

Photo Credits: Cover karelnoppe/Shutterstock.com; p. 5 Rob Lewine/Image Source/Getty Images; p. 7 imtmphoto/Shutterstock.com; p. 9 Rido/Shutterstock.com; p. 11 Syda Productions/Shutterstock.com; p. 13 Westend61/Getty Images; p. 15 Flamingo Images/Shutterstock.com; p. 17 KK Tan/Shutterstock.com; p. 19 Hero Images/DigitalVision/Getty Images; p. 21 FatCamera/E+/Getty Images; p. 22 Monkey Business Images/Shutterstock.com.

Cataloging-in-Publication Data

Names: Morlock, Rachael.
Title: I am kind online / Rachael Morlock.
Description: New York : PowerKids Press, 2020. | Series: I am a good digital citizen | Includes glossary and index.
Identifiers: ISBN 9781538349601 (pbk.) | ISBN 9781538349625 (library bound) | ISBN 9781538349618 (6pack)
Subjects: LCSH: Internet and children–Juvenile literature. | Online etiquette–Juvenile literature. | Cyberbullying–Juvenile literature.
Classification: LCC HQ784.I58 M673 2020 | DDC 004.67'8083–dc23

Manufactured in the United States of America

CPSIA Compliance Information: Batch #CSPK19. For Further Information contact Rosen Publishing, New York, New York at 1-800-237-9932.

CONTENTS

YOUR JOB ONLINE

Every time you go on a computer and **connect** to the Internet, you join a large digital world. Your job online is to be a good digital citizen. You can do this by following rules for safety and fairness. Good digital citizens also make the Internet better by being kind.

WHAT IS KINDNESS?

When you are kind, you show others you care about them. Kind people help and look out for others. They think about people's feelings. They let others know when they're thankful. Kind words and acts take many forms in the real world. There are also many ways to be kind online!

REAL PEOPLE, REAL FEELINGS

Sometimes the Internet can feel like another world or a game. Remember, there's often a real person on the other end of your online connections. Whether they're a friend or a stranger, they have thoughts and feelings, too. Be sure to treat them as if you were talking face to face.

9

KIND WORDS

You'll have many chances to share your thoughts and ideas with others online. Before you send a message or post your **opinion**, though, it's best to read it again. Would you say it in person? Could it hurt someone's feelings? How would you feel if the message was sent to you?

11

THINK FIRST

"THINK" stands for true, helpful, **inspiring**, necessary, and kind. True messages use facts. Helpful messages are clear and useful. Inspiring messages build others up. Necessary messages are needed to make things better. Kind messages show you care. If your message is all those things, then you know it's ready to send or post.

13

STOP CYBERBULLYING

Cyberbullying is when people use digital **devices** to make fun of, **embarrass**, or hurt others. Cyberbullying can be a big problem for kids. You can **protect** yourself and others by setting a good example of kindness online. When you see cyberbullying, you should also help by speaking up.

15

STAND UP!

Standing up to cyberbullying is the kind thing to do. You can tell an adult when there's a problem. You can tell bullies that their **behavior** isn't OK. You can say something nice, online or offline, to show someone who's being bullied that you care. Cyberbullying can really hurt, but kindness can help.

17

INCLUDE OTHERS

Being kind means trying to **include** others. You include others by welcoming and making room for them. If you can't include everyone in your activities, then it's best not to share those activities online right away. You wouldn't want other friends to feel left out. Save your photos or posts about your activities for later.

SPREAD KINDNESS

Kindness comes in many forms. Use your thoughtfulness and **creativity** to find different ways of being kind! You might send messages that **compliment** people you know. Or you could share tips online to help other people complete a task. Whatever you choose to do, use your time online to spread kindness.

KINDNESS COUNTS

Every time you're online, you choose how to act. Being kind can be as easy as giving a compliment or sending a smiley face to someone. Even simple acts can help someone feel cared for. Your kindness will show other kids and adults how to make the Internet a happier place for everyone.

GLOSSARY

behavior: The way someone acts.

compliment: To say nice things about someone or something.

connect: To join or link together.

creativity: The ability to make new things or think of new ideas.

device: A tool used for a certain purpose.

embarrass: To make someone feel confused and foolish.

include: To make someone a part of something.

inspiring: Moving someone to do something great.

opinion: A personal judgment or belief.

protect: To keep safe.

INDEX

WEBSITES

Due to the changing nature of Internet links, PowerKids Press has developed an online list of websites related to the subject of this book. This site is updated regularly. Please use this link to access the list: www.powerkidslinks.com/digcit/kind